I0166895

Hunt for Red Meat
(love stories)

Book 1 of the BLOOK series

Laurel McHargue

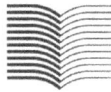

STRACK PRESS

Leadville, Colorado

Hunt for Red Meat: (love stories)

Book 1 of the BLOOK series

Published by STRACK PRESS LLC

Leadville, CO

Copyright © 2017 by Laurel McHargue. All rights reserved.

laurel@strackpress.com

No part of this publication may be reproduced or transmitted in any form or by any means, electronic, mechanical, including photocopying, or by any information storage and retrieval system without written permission from Laurel McHargue, except for the inclusion of brief quotations in a review. All images, logos, quotes, and trademarks included in this book are subject to use according to trademark and copyright laws of the United States of America.

Library of Congress Control Number: 2017909516

McHargue, Laurel, Author

Hunt for Red Meat: (love stories)

Laurel McHargue

ISBN: 978-0-9969711-9-5

Cover Design by Laurel McHargue

DEDICATION

To Mike,
for if it weren't for him,
I'd be whipping up couch potato stories!

CONTENTS

INTRODUCTION

Driving to Denver with my firstborn one day, I told him about my idea to create a book in which I could consolidate my favorite blog posts. I've written about everything from cutting my own hair to cleaning firstborn's apartment (I'll feature *that* story in my horror book), and I had the perfect title.

"I think the title will be something like, *Life and Love and Lust and Loss . . . and Hunting,*" I told him. "What do you think?"

Most people know I like one-word titles, and Nick is no exception.

"Blook," he replied.

"Blook? Blook at what?" I was confused. Knowing how adept both my sons are at pulling profound puns from mundane utterances, I didn't want to overlook an opportunity to pick up a tossed gem.

"Just Blook. A blog book. A Blook."

I think I said something goofy like, "*Noice!*" because, you know, I wanted to be cool, and I knew right away I'd have to use BLOOK in the title somehow.

There's something about the word "look" that resonates in my corpuscles (the word corpuscles, however, gives me the shivers), and I think it's because "look" was the first word I learned to read in Mrs. Brown's 1st grade classroom.

I still remember the surge of excitement I felt when I saw the letters L, O, O, K, and knew I could say the word "Look" aloud. It was magical.

So, instead of creating one huge blook with all my favorite posts, I've decided to publish a series of blooks, this one about hunting being the first.

"But 'love stories'? How can stories about hunting be love stories?" you might ask.

Well, most of these expeditions in search of the wily elk happened with my husband of over three decades, so how could they not also be about love?

Several years ago while waiting in a doctor's office I came across a contest called "America's Hottest Husband" in *Redbook Magazine.* All I had to do was write an essay of no more than 500 words and provide photos. Easy-peasy, I thought, and submitted the following essay along with several photos of Mike at his finest:

Thirty years ago I said "Yes!" to a hunky young stud I had known for less than a year. Not long after, I also agreed to marry him! Although I thought Mike was hot before I knew where life would lead us, when I look at him now, I feel a heat that can only come from years of smoldering companionship, and no, that's not just menopause talking!

What makes my man hot outside of his obvious anatomical attractiveness? His strength—the kind that says, "I will keep you safe," even when I know I can take care of myself; his kindness—which expresses the depth of his character that is even more important than his muscles; his sense of humor—even though it sometimes makes me shake my head and roll my eyes, I know that he would stand on his head for me if it would cheer me up when I'm feeling down (because he has!); his trust in me—that comes from respect and encourages me to do things like attend school reunions alone because he knows that I'll have more fun chatting with my friends without him pretending to enjoy himself; his patience—he will never say no when I want to open our home for friends and strays alike because he knows how happy it makes me; his generosity—the kind that lets me know I come first (unless I don't want to!) and does not begrudge a frivolous purchase I might "have to have"; his adventuresome nature—that spirit of bold goal-setting which first caught my interest and continually reminds me that there will always be exciting times ahead; and most importantly, his brain—his constant quest for knowledge has made him a person I love to be with, and even after 30 years of marriage, we still have stimulating things to discuss! I not only love this man, I honestly like him, too!

Mike has always respected my individuality and my dreams, and has recently encouraged me to leave a paying job to pursue my lifelong desire to write books. He helped me create and raise two remarkable sons. He thinks nothing of being called in the middle of the night to rescue lost hikers in our Colorado mountains. He left a soul-sucking corporate job to work as a public servant in our small community. He works—and works out—with a passion that inspires me, and he's neater than I am around the house. He still wears the same size as when I met him, and still looks smokin' in his camouflage hunting attire. My husband not only brings home the bacon, he also builds the fire and cooks it, sizzling hot and crispy, just like I want it. Now that's hot!

My man possesses all of the traits I find desirable in a man, and I will follow his hot little butt to the ends of the earth. He will always be America's Hottest Husband in my eyes!

Mike didn't win the *Redbook* contest, probably because the photos I sent of him were typical of how I see him at his finest—smiling and sweaty after completing some audacious race. But I think this essay helps to illustrate why hunting with a partner can engender love stories.

The stories in this blook span three years of hunting seasons in Lake County, Colorado. If you'd like to see the photos associated with each entry—and there are some pretty funny ones—go to the links I've included in each chapter.

I've also included a bonus story at the end about my first time fishing. Let's just say that my exuberance made up for my, ah, obvious inexperience!

Whether or not you're a hunter, put yourself in my camouflage pants and boots and screaming orange vest (it really does complement the camo) and experience the thrill of hunting . . . and love . . . if only through my eyes!

And yes, that's me on the cover. Best selfie I've ever staged!

~ *Laurel McHargue*

1: THE HUNT BEGINS

"A bad day hunting still beats a good day working."
~Unknown

10/29/14

> *Hunting wily elk*
> *Wilderness protects them all*
> *Caught my man instead*

Steaming sweat streamed down my spine. My 20-pound pack was plastered to my back. I had overdressed, once again, for the last day of hunting season. Or perhaps Mike was moving just a tad too fast up the endless incline, eager for success on that last day. No, I had certainly overdressed.

Although Mike hunted squirrels in his boyhood days, the only hunting I had ever done was for bargains at department stores. I had never dreamed of a day I'd be hunting elk, or any other animal, but there I was in the wilds of Colorado, excited for the shot that would guarantee us fresh meat for months. Mike had the cow tag. He would shoot, and I would do the field dressing. For days and sleepless nights I practiced in my head what I had learned on YouTube. I knew I'd be a pro.

Like Hansel and Gretel, the elk in the area left trails and trails of moist offerings for us to follow. Mike found them all, and I did my best not to complain when one trail led to another, and another, even though I suspected we were being led on a wild poop chase.

We hunted one thirteen-hour day the first weekend of the season, and although I often found myself either sweating bullets or shivering in my boots, I frequently felt just right. Those moments steeled me for subsequent excursions.

We fell into a speechless rhythm. I stopped whenever he stopped, about every eight steps. We did this for hours, and by early afternoon, even my eye muscles ached from the constant, stealthy surveillance.

Countless times I watched Mike stop, pick up a twig and stick it into a pile of elk poop. I soon learned that the shiny ones were the freshest. There was no doubt in my mind that elk had been there before us.

"Does this look familiar?" he asked me later in the day, quizzing me to test my orientation proficiency. I lied and said yes, though the poop piles were all starting to smell the same to me. I did notice a familiar twig sticking out of one pile and realized we had made a huge circle.

Hunt for Red Meat: (love stories)

In addition to coordinating our movement, we also coordinated our pee breaks. Peeing in the woods is the best. After the squat, the sweet release, a clench or two and a wiggle-waggle, I'm ready for the next expanse of forest.

Frequently, busy squirrels chattered at us to move along, though we had no interest in their tiny little nuts. We did our best to be as stealthy as our prey, but Mike had a creaky boot that I'm certain alerted the nut gatherers. Then, of course, the blast of an occasional fart would stop us both in our tracks. We would look at one another in mock surprise and mouth the word, "bugling?" It was always funny, and we found ourselves suppressing juvenile giggles every time it happened.

At one point as we were creeping through a particularly mucky draw, our boots pulling—"Shhgluck!"—from the mud, I had flashbacks to my Army reconnaissance training.

"Feels like we're in Nam," I whispered to Mike. It was a ridiculous thing to say. He rolled his eyes and shook his head.

At one point that long day as we climbed up from yet another draw, we were treated by the flash of two glorious elk cows about 30 yards away. Fortunately for them, they saw us before we recognized them. Before Mike could raise his rifle, they disappeared even faster than they had appeared, and with barely a sound.

Mike continued to zigzag us through the forest in a way I never could. I'll admit it . . . I don't know the first thing about using a GPS in the forest and would never attempt an adventure like this without him.

Later in the afternoon I began to get cranky and we stopped for a long break. Between hours of trudging in stiff boots and snacks of nothing but raisins and nuts, both my plantar fasciitis and my TMJ flared up. I considered myself

3

lucky never to have had IBS. Because I have celiac, however, the smell of the non-gluten-free beef jerky Mike was eating made my mouth water.

"Let's go up the trail a bit and find a good vantage point," he said after we finished our snack. Maybe we'll get lucky." Mike was always trying to keep my spirits high.

I could taste the jerky lingering in his whisper, and I started to drool a little.

"You could get lucky right here," I whispered back, a little more than half-joking.

"Yeah, and right as we're doing it, a whole herd would walk by," Mike said quietly, and it was all we could do to muffle our giggles. He sure did want to score an elk that day. I settled for a jerky-kiss, and we continued moving until the sun went down on that long day.

"Let's head back now," he said, disappointed, though not defeated. I had no idea where "back" was, but continued to follow my guy, still in stealth mode, into the darkness, just as we had started the day.

One evening later in the week while standing motionless, I noticed a clearing on the forest floor outlined by fallen trees. The sight transported me to the woods behind my childhood home where my best friend, my sister and I would set up pretend rooms with branches and stones. The woods were really only a few undeveloped lots, but to us, the wilderness seemed immense. We loved to bounce on a tree bent low to the ground, but never ventured too far beyond it because of the monster we were told lived there.

An enormous crow circling above us brought me back to the present. He seemed to love the sound of his own voice, and Mike and I shook our heads at the noisy ruckus. Growing chilly yet not moving at all lest we herald our presence, I realized about the only noiseless thing I could do was kegel exercises. Since those made me shiver, though, I decided to try balancing on one foot, being careful not to crunch twigs when I switched between the two.

In subsequent days we stood on high lookouts during sunsets and rises. I watched as spider webs shimmered with bits of sunlight, looking like stray strands of tinsel on discarded Christmas trees.

Despite only one other sighting of elk late one evening after legal hunting hours, we continued to hike with hope each time we went back out to hunt. Huddled against a stone-cold boulder during our last night out, our stomachs growling and shivers setting in deep, we both still thought we might get lucky on our last descent from the forest. Alas, we were mistaken.

"I think we're elkless," Mike said near the end of that last day in the wild.

"It was an awesome week," I whispered. And it was true. We hadn't had so much quiet time together in years. When we were out there, we had no TV, no politics, no talk of Ebola. No elk? No problem. Much hunting happened, though at the end of the week, the only kill was a pesky gnat I successfully snatched from its orbit around my drippy nose one afternoon.

"And don't forget," I continued, "my hunting season starts next weekend!"

After spending days trudging through the woods with my husband on our first ever hunting expedition, I concluded that trying to find an elk in a jillion acres of national forest is even harder than trying to find a pair of reading glasses in your house. You know there are lots of them around, but they're never where someone claims to have spotted them recently.

We may have ended the week elkless, but the experience brought me closer to the man who grew up raised by wolves in the wilderness of northern California—a story I tell everyone I meet about him. But that's a story for another day.

For more photos, go to: http://leadvillelaurel.com/hunting-with-my-hubby/

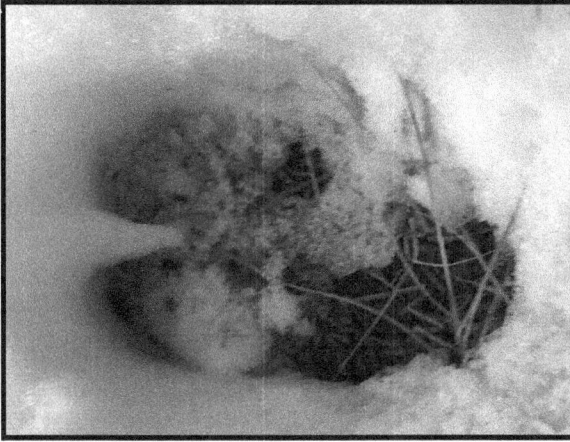

2: GAL'S GOT THE GUN

> "There is a passion for hunting something deeply
> implanted in the human breast."
> ~Charles Dickens

Day 1: 11/3/14

> *He trusts me to walk*
> *Behind him with loaded gun*
> *Crazy husband, mine*

Since I began my "Hunting with Hubby" story with a haiku, I figured I should do the same for my week of hunting. Although I was able to take lots of notes with my iPhone (on airplane mode, of course!) while following Mike for days and days last week, I do not have the same luxury this week as I am the one carrying the Sako .308 elk-slayer. Therefore, instead of waiting until the end of the week to gather my notes into one story, I'll do my best to capture the highlights of "My Turn to Bag the Wily Elk" each day. I have until 5:29 p.m. on November 9th to accomplish this.

We started before sunrise yesterday in an area we were told had lots of activity. We covered tons of terrain and I found myself dressed too warmly again. Since I was in the lead this time, however, I got to choose when and where to stop, and I took lots of cool-down and pee breaks. The most exciting activity we experienced ended up being two frisky squirrels bolting out of a nearby tree chasing one another, and one nearly running up my well-camouflaged leg! It took everything in my power not to jump and scream like a little girl, even though there were no elk within earshot.

The day was gorgeous and Mike did his best to locate the source of tidbits left on trails, but to no avail.

Here's my haiku from yesterday's attempt:

No beginner's luck
Humming "Kumbayah, my elk"
Only squirrels come

~ ~ ~

Day 2: 11/4/14

We started the hunt this morning feeling hopeful. With the extra hour of sleep (why are we still observing Daylight Saving Time?) and anticipation that the light snowfall would make it easy to find our tasty temptress (I, too, have a cow tag), we set out to a new location.

Hours later with much terrain covered following teasing signs on trails, we returned to the vehicle, elkless again. The spider webs that yesterday glinted with sunshine today were like strands of snow pearls hanging from the trees. Not too far from the road, we found evidence of elk in the area.

This morning's haiku:

> *Snow frosted elk skull*
> *Successful kill for someone*
> *Sorry it's not mine*

Along with the skull were the pelvic bones and spine, all white as the snow that soon would bury them.

Knowing that we would find easy trails in the snow, we returned to the same spot this afternoon. With me in the lead and feeling like this could be "it," I did my best to ignore the loud scrunching of our boots as we forged forward into the forest. At first it was humorous, but with each step, my boots became heavier and heavier until I could kick off the mounting platform. I felt a bit like Frankenstein.

> *Frankenstein trudges*
> *Hiking boots laden with snow*
> *Scaring elk away*

After a couple of hours of seeing nothing but rabbit and squirrel tracks, I started to get a little irritated. I was tired. I was hungry. I was making far too much noise in the winter wonderland of woods and caved-in mine shafts to sneak up on any prey. It was snowing, the sun was setting, and all I really wanted to do was go home and enjoy a glass of wine. Screw the wily elk.

Mike could tell I was starting to feel petulant and took the lead, trusting me to follow him, on slippery surfaces, with a loaded rifle. When he suggested that we crest one more hill to "see what was on the other side," I almost cried. Instead, I turned around.

"See?" he whispered. "We're doing *real* hunting. There aren't too many people seeing this view tonight." And he was right. We decided then to go just a bit further before heading back home.

Not 20 feet away we found a fresh track, an elk track in the snow heading downhill. With adrenaline pumping, we followed the trail down and down and down . . . and down some more and around . . . until it stopped, right by a large pine tree. I looked up. No elk in the tree. It was truly time to head home.

By the time we reached our vehicle, it was quite dark. The rising moon shone through the foggy haze of rolling clouds and melting snow.

Perhaps tomorrow will be "it," the day I will bring down my first elk. If not, I'll just have to suffer through my spectacular surroundings a little longer.

For more photos, go to: http://leadvillelaurel.com/hunting-haikus-and-more-days-1-and-2/

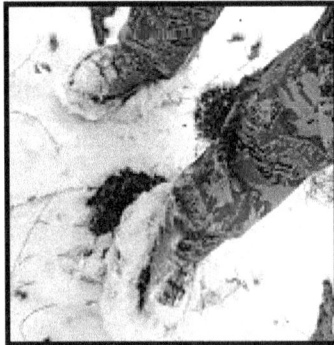

3: ALONE

"I do not hunt for the joy of killing but for the joy of living, and the inexpressible pleasure of mingling my life however briefly, with that of a wild creature that I respect, admire and value." ~John Madson

Day 3

Don't try this at home
Shouldn't go hunting alone
I went anyway

Since Mike had to travel for the next few days and my writing buddy was horrified by the idea of going hunting with me (my invitation startled her speechless), I was forced to make a decision. Either give up on a perfectly good evening of hunting (my morning was booked), or go by myself. I realized—as I was making it—that it was a foolish decision. My internal mother-voice was screaming, "Don't be a moron! What do you think you're doing?"

But I had to do it. I had to see if I had the guts to go it alone, just me, my pack, and the elk-slayer. I've recently found myself wondering about age-related things, like, when was it that I stopped working on my handstands? I used to be pretty good at doing them. Sure, I may be 55, but Jack LaLanne was doing his insane workouts until the week before he died at age 96! Yes, I had to go hunting by myself. I would only be out for a couple of hours, and I would head home before the sun set. Maybe I would even try a handstand against a wall when I got home.

Halfway up the rocky, snowy road I started to get nervous and ate the third of six "fun size" Snickers bars I would consume just getting to the trailhead. Although I probably should have lost several pounds with all the hunting and hiking I've done these last couple of weeks, I've used the increase in energy expenditure to justify my over-indulgence in the chocolaty treats.

In any case, my "what ifs" were going into overdrive. What if I get stuck? How would I turn my 4-Runner around on the steep, narrow, icy trail? What if my brakes won't work on the way back down? I had myself worked into a tizzy and almost turned around at a wide area on the ascent, but I couldn't give up that easily. With a half-mile to go before I could hunt, my tires spun in a rut. "Shit," I whispered, as if I would scare away a potential target if I had said it any louder.

I was able to back up—Phew!—and decided I probably shouldn't drive any farther. I parked off-trail and geared up. "Shit," I whispered again when I realized I had left my gloves at home. Alas, all I could find in my normally-well-stocked vehicle was a pair of blue rubber-coated garden gloves. "Perhaps this is telling you something," my mother-voice whispered. I ignored it and stuck the silly gloves into my pocket.

The surge of adrenaline I experienced when I loaded the .308 surprised me, and for a brief moment I thought I might have to rush to the woods to unload, um, the Snickers bars. The feeling passed, however, and I started down the slippery trail with the stealthiest steps I could manage. I saw many tracks crossing the road. Bunnies. Squirrels. Birds. I couldn't remember what mountain lion tracks looked like, but I was pretty sure I didn't see any of those.

I stopped frequently as I maneuvered down the trail and practiced a sighting drill my friend John taught me. Look at the target, keep both eyes open and on target, bring the weapon up so the scope is in line with your sighting eye, and voilà! Ready to fire! I got better and faster each time I practiced. That sitting squirrel had no idea how cute he looked in my crosshairs.

When I finally reached the area where we had hunted on Day 1, I settled down in a spot with good visibility in several directions. The blue rubber gloves proved to be most unsatisfactory, but I had grabbed a couple of expired hand-warmer packets from my vehicle and they provided a bit of heat.

For the next half-hour I sat in silence as the sun settled into the trees. I knew there would be no reckless herds of elk wandering across my path with "Shoot me!" signs on their sides, and if there had been, I probably would have shot photos. What was I thinking, hunting alone?

I brushed the snow off my butt and started back up to my vehicle, practicing my aiming skills every few minutes along the way. I could have continued to hunt for another hour, but I wanted to make the drive back while there was still some ambient light. I couldn't resist taking a snow-selfie. Roger Miller's song "King of the road" played in my head when I saw my impressive shadow on the snowy surface. It was better than my pesky mother-voice.

When I spotted my vehicle, I felt like I had accomplished something. I had overcome my fear of doing something risky at my age and alone.

The rising moon and setting sun were the spoils of my hunt.

I took my time driving down the mountain. When I got home, I tried a handstand. Next time I won't use the door.

For more photos, go to: http://leadvillelaurel.com/hunting-day-3/

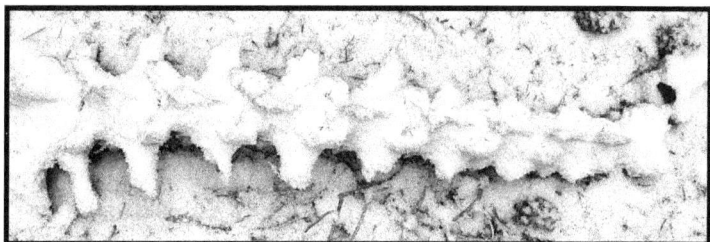

4: HOPE AND HUMOR

"Vegetarians are cool. All I eat are vegetarians— except for the occasional mountain lion steak." ~Ted Nugent

Day 6

Another peaceful
Morning alone in the woods
Wish elk would visit

Before the sun rose this morning, the full moon rolled over the edge of Mt. Massive with startling speed. After the confidence boost I got from my solo evening hunt, I decided to try my luck one more time before Mike returned. Not normally a morning person, I was proud of myself for getting up and out before the town awoke, especially since I had barely slept last night. I spent most of the night ruminating about what I would do if I actually saw a potential target, and if I was successful, how I would position myself for my first-kill-selfie.

I need not have ruminated. For three and a half hours I meandered through an area suggested by a friend, and although I spent most of the time in wooded areas, I never strayed too far from points I could identify. After all, I didn't have my hunting buddy with me, and hadn't yet learned how to use my GPS in the wild.

I enjoyed taking my time exploring things that caught my eye: the base of an old television, a mysterious hanging bucket, a tin can cemetery, beautiful feathers left from a more successful hunter's meal, and although I came home without seeing anything larger than a squirrel, the experience left me feeling happier than if I had stayed at home and slept a few more hours, something I will do right about now.

For more photos, go to: http://leadvillelaurel.com/hunting-day-6/

~ ~ ~

Day 7

Lost my funny bone
"Signs, signs, everywhere there's signs"
But that's about all

Yup. If finally happened. I lost my sense of humor this morning.

Mike and I were back where we had hunted last weekend, where I had silently cursed the endless inclines, where a friend—just the day after we were there—harvested an elk. "Harvest: to catch, take, or remove for use." Sounds far more acceptable than "shot," eh?

Anyway, we both felt like this would be our lucky day. It was time, I reasoned. Sure, I knew statistics were against us and only about 25% of hunters successfully filled their tags each season, but we had been doing more than due diligence!

The day was clear and not too cold. I was surprised by the comfort of the pack on my back and the rifle in my hands. My weeks of putting in the hours were paying off.

After almost two hours of sleuthing, nature made an insistent call.

"I reeeally need to go!" I whispered to Mike after peeling off my top jacket. With the sun up, the day was growing warm.

"Did you bring paper?" he whispered back.

"No, I'll just use a stick," I said.

"Gross," he responded.

"You're a baby," I said.

When I finished—one of those magical experiences that didn't even require a stick!—I felt light on my feet despite the weight in my pack, which felt just a bit weightier than when I had donned it earlier. Nevertheless, we were back to sleuthing and still felt confident.

But hours passed. Yes, the day was lovely. Yes, I was spending time with my husband. And yes, regardless of the day's outcome, I was in a place with no laundry to fold, no dishes to wash, no bills to pay. So why did I start to lose my sense of humor?

I did my best to accept Mike's suggestions for which trail to follow next even though they inevitably led back up increasingly steep hills. I hate steep hills. I hate steep hills with a passion. I've lived at 10,200' for eight years now and I still get winded climbing the stairs at home.

So I really tried not to resent his suggestions and his ability to climb steep hills like a mountain goat. But it was becoming more difficult. My head was telling me, "He wants to find an elk as badly as you do, so pull up your big-girl panties and drive on," but my body was screaming, "Hello! I'm sending you signs! This is hurting me as much as it's hurting you!"

Something ran across the crest of a hill when I was about to throw down my weapon and pout. That was all it took to get me moving again, even though Mike and I both agreed it was probably a deer.

Into the fifth hour of beating around the bush, however, in addition to the stabbing plantar fasciitis in my left heal, I started feeling like I was developing trigger-elbow in my right arm and stock-wrist in my left from holding my weapon at-the-ready for so long.

Five hours of being "at-the-ready," of anticipating the moment I would crest the final hill and see a whole herd of elk just chillin' on the other side, of studying each step before I took it, suddenly took its toll.

I used to think I might actually have a moment of hesitation before pulling the trigger if I were ever to get an elk in my crosshairs, but no more. I wanted to scream, "Make my day, wily momma! Make my frickin day!"

"My fun meter is pegged," I whispered to Mike, and he agreed that it might be time to head back home for something to eat and maybe even a nap. We'd try again in the evening.

It seemed to take forever to get back to the car. *Screw these stealthy steps*, I thought, and practically stomped down one of the many hills we had climbed earlier. When we were almost out of the woods, we came across the elk bones we had seen frosted with snow the first weekend of hunting.

"I want the spine," I told Mike.

"Seriously?" he asked.

"Yup," I said.

"What are you going to do with it?" he asked.

"Probably hang it on a wall," I said. And with that, he wrapped it in a plastic bag and carried it out for me, and my petulance disappeared.

After a monster-sized brunch and a snooze, we followed a friend to a place he knew had roaming herds, and although we came home empty-handed again, the location was hill-less and I was happy. We'll go back out tomorrow because . . .

There were lots of signs!

For more photos, go to:
http://leadvillelaurel.com/hunting-day-7/

5: ONE YEAR DOWN

"If God didn't want men to hunt, he wouldn't have given him plaid shirts." ~Johnny Carson

Day 8: Morning

> *Running out of time*
> *One more hunting day remains*
> *Elk laugh knowingly*

Ranger looked up at me this morning with an expression that said, "Who are you and what have you done with my mom?" He has not been pleased with these days of pre-sunup excitement, and this morning's 04:50 alarm was just too much. He skulked back to bed.

Mike and I were on site and I was ready to shoot even before the moment it would be legal. The moon was still high over the mountains, and it was bitter cold even though I was dressed like an Eskimo. We thought we might stake out a place we had identified last night, but after standing motionless for almost 15 minutes, our toes started to freeze and even I agreed I'd rather be hiking.

We moved at a noiseless pace, and I finally felt like a *real* hunter. Having to control each foot placement helped to generate body heat. Moment by moment our surroundings unfolded with the nearly imperceptible brightening of the sky right before sunrise.

Two glorious mule deer sprang across an opening to our front, about 50 meters away, and my heart raced. I wondered if mule deer hung out with elk, but I hadn't come across that in any of my pre-hunting-season research. Still, I took it as a good sign.

For two hours we scoured the forest and poked at poop-piles, me and my shadow, until we had completed a sizeable circuit ending back at the vehicle.

"I'd say we go home, get some breakfast, and maybe come back later," said my shadow. It was unlike Mike to call it quits so quickly, but then he moved past the vehicle. "Maybe one more traverse down that way," he said, and I felt like he had read my mind.

"Sounds good," I said, still in a whisper.

"We don't have to move as stealthily this time," he whispered back.

Roger that, I thought. "Okay," came out of my mouth.

We spent another half-hour hiking and hoping the herds of sleepy elk would somehow find their way to us and sacrifice one of their own to our cause, but I guess that's just not how it happens.

Stay tuned for tonight's episode of "Looking for Luck in All the Wrong Places"!

For more photos, go to: http://leadvillelaurel.com/1124/

Hunting: Day 8 Evening

Running out of ways
To say we're elkless again
But still having fun

Or *are we?* Sure we are. And honestly, I can't believe the weather we've had this week. Sadly, it's weather that doesn't motivate herds of elk to come out of the mountains for warmth.

Ranger did his best to prevent me from leaving this evening, and the text message I received from one of my four sisters—"Why don't you just drink wine like the rest of us . . . wtf?"—almost made me reconsider our evening hunt.

But I can't end this week saying, "I'll bet we would have bagged one if we had gone out that 8th night." And so off we went to a location near the death-by-hills area. I drove the trusty 4-Runner up inclines I wasn't sure it could handle, white-knuckled the whole way up.

"If you have a long shot," Mike whispered to me when we were close to the top of the world, "I'll bend over and you can brace yourself on my back."

I swear, the man really must love me.

"Um, yeah, no. Don't think I'll be doing that," I whispered back as gratefully as I could. Although we saw many perfect places for elk to hang out at the end of the day, thick patches of willows everywhere, we never saw a sign of habitation. Not even by a long shot.

Driving back down at the end of the evening made me realized just how far we had climbed on our previous hunts, and once I could release my death-grip on the steering wheel, I was able to bask in the glory of my physical accomplishments.

And now we're down to one more day. Back at home I saw myself in the hall mirror and laughed. I asked Mike, "So tell me, honestly, does this pack make my ass look fat?"

Giggles.

For more photos, go to: http://leadvillelaurel.com/hunting-day-8-evening/

~ ~ ~

Day 9

> *Here's my epilogue*
> *They were somewhere, I was naught*
> *Never heard a herd*

Although I never pulled the trigger, no one can say I didn't give it my best shot. I ended this hunting season as I began it—elkless—but richer, still, for the experience.

Mike and I watched another magical morning bloom across the sky as we moved through our last hunting area of the season. Knowing that this was our last day, my last chance to do something I've lost sleep over these past several weeks, we walked more slowly than ever. Even so, the "scrunch" of dry snow and ice under our boots was too loud.

We agreed that if we saw nothing this morning, we'd call it quits for the day. We whispered little. When we did, it was the usual, "This would be a great place for them to hide," followed by, "Yeah, I know, they should *be* here," followed by, "They're probably peeing on our car right now," followed by muffled chuckles. It really was comical, or sad, depending on your perspective. I'll go with comical.

Day after day of prodding poop piles (a band name, perhaps?) made me recall a story my dad used to enjoy telling, the one about two little boys sent to play in a room filled with horse shit for a day. When they got home, the mom asked about their day. One boy cried and complained about all the poop. The other boy gleefully exclaimed his willingness to return the next day because "with all that horse poo, there must be a pony in there somewhere"!

The only real "signs" we saw today, however, were signs of disrespectful hunters, and that made us both angry. I'll never understand why anyone would think it's okay to leave beer cans and bottles littering the outdoors. I hoped they went home elkless as well.

When we reached the farthest point in our search, it was time to head back home. We both decided there was no need for stealth, and had we been the hunted, we would have made easy targets. It was a bizarre thought, I know, but it did cross my mind as we hustled back noisily to the 4-Runner. Too many "Hunger Games" movies, I suppose.

By the time we returned home, I decided I would return to a close-in site for the last few hours of the day.

"I'll go by myself," I told Mike, not wanting him to feel obligated to watch the ball drop, so to speak, on my first hunting season.

"Why would you do that?" he asked. "Of course I'm going with you." He looked at me as if I'd grown an extra nose.

So without going into the step by step details, the most exciting moment of the evening was when I caught movement in the trees behind us. I spun around and put my scope on the biggest rabbit I have ever seen.

"Don't shoot the rabbit with the .308," said Mike matter-of-factly.

"Oh, but—" I protested. The sun was disappearing over the mountains and I was hungry. And did I say it was the biggest rabbit I had ever seen? It wasn't elk-size, of course, but it would have made quite a stew.

I sure did want to end my hunting blog with a thrilling conclusion and photos of me elbows deep in the guts of my first kill. But it just wasn't meant to be.

I did, however, confirm what we have known all along. Those wily beasts have been following us . . . and laughing.

For more photos, go to: http://leadvillelaurel.com/hunting-day-9-epilogue/

(Those are *not* chocolate chips. Don't worry. I wore gloves.)

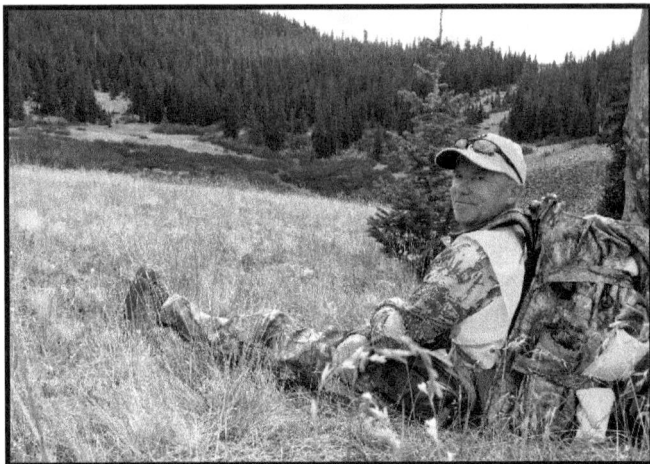

6: YEAR TWO ADVENTURES

"The No. 1 rule in duck hunting is to go where the ducks are." ~Jase Robertson

Day 1

Here are some tips on what to do before charging out on Day 1 of your hunting season:

1. Read last year's hunting blog and laugh about how inexperienced you were.
2. Tell yourself, "This will be the year!"
3. Review videos on the gutless method of harvesting your kill, preferably while you're eating something.

4. Tell yourself, "I can do that in 10 minutes, 15 minutes max."
5. Don't worry about losing sleep the night before Day 1. You won't have any trouble sleeping after 8 hours of moving, sweating, waiting, and shivering.
6. Assure your non-hunting friends you do realize you're stopping a beating heart when you shoot an animal.
7. Practice whispering with your hunting partner. Start with little messages like, "They're waiting for us."
8. Ask everyone where they bagged their elk. When they tell you, go somewhere else.

Mike and I started our Day 1 hunt before sunrise on Mt. Zion because we heard that's where our next meal would be hanging out. Despite my initial dread of spending a day beating the brush after re-reading my post from last year's hunting adventures, I geared up and we got to our parking spot before sunrise. Mike knew my mobility was limited since I just ditched the crutches a week ago from ankle surgery six weeks prior and convinced me we'd move at my speed.

It didn't take long before we found our hunting rhythm, which truly illustrated "a snail's pace." Although we saw some signs (signs=poop) of elk having been there, we were not convinced they were still hanging around. After many hours and much hiking and beautiful places where they *should* have been, we returned home at midday. We knew when we went back out that evening, we'd find them.

Driving back a different starting spot on the mountain, still full of adrenaline and eager to fill our tags on Day 1, we discussed what would happen if we came across a "twofer." Mike has a cow tag and I have a bull tag, same season, so the idea of walking into a pasture and catching a little bull-on-cow action was just too funny not to consider.

Alas, our anticipation adrenaline wore off as the sun set, and we returned home again, home again, jiggety-jig, to a dinner of mac and cheese and early to bed. Day 2 would be the day.

~ ~ ~

Day 2

We heard that Weston Pass was the place to go to find our wily elk for sure. So instead of heeding my tip #8 for Day 1 prep, we drove up to a spot on the road below Weston Pass way before the sun rose.

The hike up to where we knew the elk would be was arduous (for someone like me with a gimpy ankle), but we made good time and enjoyed the sight of dawn breaking over the cold Rocky Mountains. After a while, we hunkered down in some pine trees. We'd wait a while and watch the herds pass by. We'd have our pick of tasty future meals.

After about half an hour, Mike decided to move farther up the hill. I stayed below. We'd have different vantage points of the same open area through which the elk would meander . . . at any minute. I drilled myself on the gutless method of removing the tenderloins. Dinner.

Suddenly I saw wild gesticulations from above, and when I followed Mike's pointed finger, THERE THEY WERE! Although difficult to see from my position, a cow, two calves and a spike were walking through a small clearing between thick pines on the far, far side of the meadow. Mike gestured for me to come up to where he was already in a firing position, but I think we both knew that the tiny window of opportunity and the distance were too challenging to overcome in the split second between seeing them and watching them disappear.

"I should've taken the shot," he said, "but by the time I had the elevation adjusted, it was too late."

"You did the right thing. You want a clean shot." I told him what he already knew.

"You stay here. I'm going over to see if I can pick up the trail."

For the next 90 minutes, Mike hiked and I lay prone in the meadow grass by a large, dead tree trunk. Maybe he'd scare them out and I'd get my shot. Instead, I waited and lounged and peered through the grass, remembering my 5th grade teacher at Archie T. Morrison Elementary School in Braintree who had us do something quite similar during our poetry unit, but without rifles. I think she might have been the one who sparked my interest in writing.

While Mike hiked, I shot photos, something my friends keep telling me I should be doing rather than shooting animals. I took my hunting glamour shot and visited for a while with a nosy lark bunting. I really do like shooting photos, but I'd like to know I could feed myself during the zombie apocalypse too.

By the time Mike returned, he was beat and I was ready to head home.

"There are tons of signs over there. It's like an elk highway. We'll come back tomorrow, okay?"

I would have agreed to anything at that point. We were silent as we drove home, tired and hungry, and our reward for our efforts on Day 2 was a glorious rainbow embracing our little town of Leadville.

Clearly, Day 3 would be "the day."

~ ~ ~

Day 3: 10/29/15

Once again we chose to ignore my hunting tip #8 (Ask everyone where they bagged their elk. When they tell you, go somewhere else) and arrived at our pull-off below Weston Pass even earlier than on Day 2. As it was pitch black and I was uncertain of my footing, Mike carried my rifle in his pack for the steepest section of our approach until dawn broke and it was time to chamber a round. He's the awesomest husband I know.

KIND bars have been our snack of choice for a few years now, and although Mike has never been an early morning breakfast eater (I must eat in the morning or I become an ogre), he snarfed a couple down before our ascent. The resultant gastric consequences provided hilarity soon thereafter.

"Did you hear something?" he whispered to me with a big smile halfway up the hill. "It sounded like bugling!"

I rolled my eyes as I would do numerous times over the next hour while the nutritious bars wreaked havoc with his digestion. So much bugling. But I don't blame *him* for scaring away our potential dinner.

I blame the monkey crow. I wish I'd thought to tap the record button on my iPhone when we heard him. Snow flurries were soft in the tree line, and because my ankle was feeling pretty good, I decided to stay with Mike as he traversed the higher grounds rather than loll about in the meadow where our elk really should have been.

The crow's laughter was an even closer imitation of monkey chatter than Mike can imitate, and we stopped to enjoy the merriment for a moment before continuing our stealthy trudge through and over thick and downed pines. Soft little Christmas trees with snow-sprinkled new growth sprouted where the old had fallen long ago, and well into our ascent, Mike stopped for a break. He's always thinking of me, but I could tell he was also beginning to get discouraged.

Within moments of hitting the trail again, I paused for a familiar routine. I knew he'd spotted a sign. Sure enough, there it was. Fudge-brownie-fresh poop.

We had already traversed too far for my comfort. My ankle was beginning to ache (I'd been telling myself that hunting is good physical therapy after surgery, but at that point I was questioning myself) and I started praying to Diana, Artemis, Orion, all of the hunting deities, to hide the poopers.

Because "they" listened to me, we hiked and hiked, and hiked and hiked, until we came to another huge clearing far beyond and above the meadow I suddenly wished I had stayed in.

"Look. Classic *Field and Stream* terrain," Mike whispered. "This is where it says they *should* be." We've repeated this same message to one another in several locations already. It's become a joke.

"I know, but elk don't read," I whispered back.

"Elk racist," he replied. Muffled giggling ensued.

We crept around the enormous open space and I realized that not only were there no more signs of elk anymore, but my ankle was seriously unhappy. And we were seriously far and high above where we'd parked. And we'd been out for hours and hours and I was ready to become a pescatarian. I like to fish. I like to eat fish. Fishing is easy. I can sit down while I fish. Fishing rods aren't that heavy. I can drive really close to where I want to fish.

"You stay here and rest. I'm going back into the trees over there and if I don't see anything, we'll head back."

I was all about the heading back, but also truly concerned about the terrain. From where I stood, I couldn't see over the edge of the field. I had no idea how steep our descent would be. So after having him take the last photo in which I could smile that day, I leaned against a downed tree with my feet uphill and did my best to remain optimistic. And that's when I had a most unexpected visitor.

An elk? Not a chance. But at the spot where I landed in the acres and acres of terrain we'd covered that day was one little ladybug. For the next half hour as Mike searched for our elusive prey, she and I visited. I marveled at her resolve to stay with me, figuring it was because my body was far warmer than anything in that wind-whipped field. She made me smile, and by the time I had to set her free, I had steeled my mind for the final trudge.

Without going into great detail, suffice it to say that my husband once again was my hero. He took my weapon from me and found a hiking stick to assist with the worst downhill journey of my life so far. I had to do several sections on my butt, so instead of crying (which I almost did several times), I gave thanks for the up-and-downstairs-butt-technique I had mastered in our house while on crutches just weeks before.

The descent was grueling, but the day was filled with beauty. And I had spent it with my man. We had no elk for all our efforts, but we were still together, still able to smile at the beauty of our surroundings, and still confident that Day 4 would be "the day."

~ ~ ~

Last Days

Spoiler alert! They're still wily, and we've not yet given up (all) hope. We decided to catch up on work and house and life in the a.m. before heading out to hunt elk on Day 4. It felt SOOO good to sleep in! We realized, of course, that our elk were frolicking in the open fields of yesterday's hunt.

Ever forgetful of tip #8, our p.m. hunt took us to another place where "people" had seen elk. The Little Union Creek area was spookily quiet, and not a hint of a breeze could muffle the crinkly crisp crunch of dried aspen leaves beneath our boots before we got into the thick trees. Tattletale squirrels shouted at us from every corner, kind of like the monkey crow on Day 3, and I delighted in sticking my tongue out at them. Simple pleasures.

Deep into the forest, I enjoyed the satisfying sound of old pine needles on the damp trails as our boots rolled over them. We found a wonderful place where the elk should have been, and while I leaned against a huge tree waiting for them in the growing silent darkness, I found myself holding my breath.

Driving home that evening we decided that our elk have most likely been camouflaging themselves in cow costumes this whole time. Or horse costumes. And they're certainly mocking us. Mike has their dialogue down pat:

"You know, someone really ought to tell them about those vests. They're glowing, for Chrissake. We can see 'em a mile away. Check it out, Clyde, they think they're invisible."

We may come home elkless, but we always find ways to laugh.

On Day 5 Mike left me on a grassy knoll—because we've heard you can get great shots from there—for 76 minutes while he scouted higher terrain. I had a fantastic field of view in every direction and the location was perfect for an elk hangout.

Not long after he left, guttural grunting sounds reverberated from a spot in a thicket not far across the path we had climbed. It's amazing what a shot of adrenaline will do to dissipate a chill in a body. I proceeded to hold my breath for the next thirty-two minutes, willing the grunters to cross my path.

Wouldn't Mike be happy to see me slicing up our next meal when he returns! But no. We worked the area another hour, finding fresh evidence of deer where I'd heard the noise, and were rewarded by finding a bizarre little outhouse in the wild on our return trip.

That afternoon at Mitchell Creek and Wurts Ditch I inhaled the wet, earthy, sweet smell of decaying pine and moss. Several snow flurries tried to take center stage, but it was too warm for them to last.

There were so many beautiful meadows for elk! Why weren't they not there! Ingrates, I think.

I knew all my friends were rooting for the elk, partly because they don't believe in hunting, partly because they don't want to believe I'd pull the trigger.

Despite the wily elk's masterful avoidance of us, being out with Mike is always my best reward. He did his best elk impersonation in an Italian accent—I have no idea why he decided they were Italian—on the way home and cracked me up. We saw horses lounging everywhere as we drove, and wondered if our elk might be wearing horse costumes.

"Hey, we're just making s'mores. Don't shoot us! Come have a s'more with us!" Mike's interpretation of the inner dialogue of hunted elk would make for a great children's story.

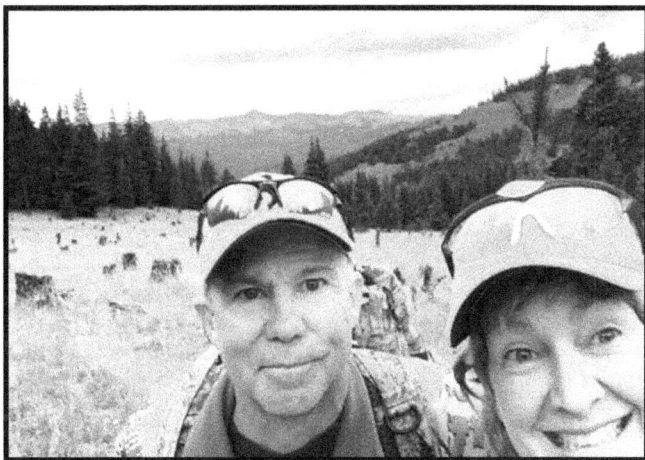

Day 7

I imagine muffled bubbles popping, like farts in a bathtub. That's the sound our boots make as we cross the field and slink through cold, frosty sage. With rosy cheeks and runny noses, we climb high on the south aspect of Taylor overlooking South Eagle Creek and it's a true winter wonderland. We hike in a couple of miles and it's bitter cold when we stop.

I take shelter under a large tree while Mike scouts higher. We passed a couple of hunters down lower in the easy terrain, and they're gone by the time we head back.

When the morning sun breaks through, snow-laden trees fling their burdens at us as we drive away.

We head back to Weston Pass in the afternoon because we just refuse to believe it's not the ideal place for wily elk to romp. We are dismayed that other hunters have taken "our spot," so we climbandclimbandclimbandclimb some more.

We take a moment to appreciate the gorgeous views of the range at dusk before we head back, discouraged but happy to be together.

"I'm out of ideas," says Mike. We're not even going to set an alarm for tomorrow.

~ ~ ~

Day 8

I woke at 5:30 without my alarm, but seeing Mike still asleep, I happily rolled over and fell back into a bizarre dream of swimming in a river overgrown with vegetation. Must have been from all that hiking through snowy sage last night.

Anyway, by the time I rose at 7:00, Mike was ready to head out, and it was clear he had decided to go it alone. My feeling ranged from joy (because it was only 20 degree out and I would have time to write and rest my ankle and get a fire going) to disappointment (because I've been with him on every outing and I like being with him and laughing with him and seeing the beauty of our surrounding and peeing in the wild).

He's going to a place we haven't been yet, to Prospect Mountain. "It's really rough," he said before he left. He's concerned about my ankle. Still, if he does happen to fill his tag (i.e., "harvest" his elk, where harvest=kill), he'll be texting me to drive up the mountain. I'm the one responsible for the ultimate slicing and dicing of our future meals because after watching several videos of the process, it didn't stick with him. I feel like I could pass a butcher's test today.

I'll be stressed until he texts or returns.

~ ~ ~

Mike returned, another season ends elkless, so we pack away our screaming orange vests and hats and tell ourselves, "Next year."

At least we are able to say that we have done much hunting. And we're still together.

For more photos, go to:: http://leadvillelaurel.com/hunting-in-colorado-day-2/

7: THIRD YEAR'S A CHARM?

"Go afield with a good attitude, with respect for the forest and fields in which you walk. Immerse yourself in the outdoor experience. It will cleanse your soul and make you a better person." ~Fred Bear

11/15/16

walk with me while I reflect on our third year of hunting the wily elk in a not-quite-stream-of-consciousness style. I'll use punctuation, but I'll make no effort to turn this into an essay. If I didn't use punctuation, I'll would look like Ill, and I'll get to that next.

I return from a week in Maine in time for my hunting week and try not to think about how much it's going to suck going from sea level to Leadville level. And I never-ever get sick, but I picked up a cold from a snotty-coughy-cute kid who sat next to me on the plane. I feel like I'm in a tunnel. But I *will* hunt the wily elk.

We're up at 4:30 a.m. and I hate getting out of bed in the morning because it's dark and cold and I have a cold and I'm in a dark cold tunnel in my head.

I'm less nervous this year, maybe because I already have two unsuccessful hunting seasons under my belt. Or maybe it's my cold medicine. Mike hesitates, asks if I'm sure I want to go because I'm a snot machine and making noises like a grunting snorting bull elk. Maybe it'll help.

We go. Our high sky is infinite black behind comets and constellations and a half-moon. The Big Dipper looms on the horizon spilling good luck onto our heads and under all of this majesty, I pee behind a bush. My cheeks are cold. All of them.

We climb. I'm happy not to be in too much pain, and what a difference a year makes after ankle surgery last year, but after a week at sea level, I'm sucking wind up the formidable Weston Pass trail. Once we get to the top, the sweet, cold, piney aroma of the waking earth fills my senses.

Blackness turns to purple turns to barely blue against a powerful pink before all fades to light, and when I can no longer see the stars, the moon overhead sparkles on the icy grasses we crunch upon. Mike is solely focused on the trail, finding tracks, finding elk poop—some even spreadable—that shows only they were here once but are here no longer. I'm focused on this blog and writing sentences in my head like, "Daylight greets us like a fond memory."

No signs of anything alive but us. As much as I want to hunker down and wait for a herd to pass—because they *should* be here, they always *should* be in the perfect places we stealthily approach—it's too cold for that. My nose runs in the cold and I'm a snot-rocket factory.

We each do our 22 push-ups for veteran suicide awareness (#22kill campaign) and head back to the truck, willing a herd or even just one tasty treat to cross our path. It doesn't happen. We sigh, heavily.

In the evening we hike around Mt. Zion. "We'll zigzag," Mike says, but I know how Mike zigzags and how many punctuations of straight ups there'll be and when we get to the fifth or sixth or seventh straight up and it's starting to get dark, I pout. I struggle to think of an analogy for what we're doing because it'll take my mind off pouting.

Trying to find a wily elk in endless acres of forest and valleys and ridgelines and mountain sides is like trying to find the one sane almond in a nuthouse. It's nearly impossible and quite possibly futile. Especially since almonds rarely talk.

There.

I want to laugh when Mike's pack catches on a dead limb and its release results in a cartoonish "BOING" sound. And then we both hear a sound that stops us in our tracks. Suddenly all senses are on fire and I'm barely breathing. Even my snot stops running.

"Move r-e-a-l-l-y slowly now," Mike whispers, and we head toward the animal sound. Half of me hopes it's nothing because it would be a bitch to get something big out of these trees at night. The other half wants to get something big out of these trees. We move like molasses in winter toward the patch of trees waiting to hear our prey and there it is again!

Simultaneously, we look up.

No, no elk in the treetops, but the rubbing of one dead tree against another in the blustery breeze makes a sound much like a large, grunting animal.

We end the day—and every day this hunting season—as we begin it, with stars and various moons emerging against darkness, more beautiful than any painting on black velvet.

And "Darkness greets us like a black velvet hug."

For more photos, go to: http://leadvillelaurel.com/hunting-3-0/

8: ROADKILL CALL

"Hunting, fishing, drawing, and music occupied my every moment. Cares I knew not, and cared naught about them." ~John James Audubon

When Mike's phone rings at 2:30 a.m.—or any other cold, dark hour—I anticipate the worst. His official job title is Lake County Emergency Manager, but he also volunteers for our county Search and Rescue team. Someone's probably lost in the mountains.

"What's that again?" Mike's oh-dark-thirty voice sounds confused. He flips on the light and I pull the covers over my head like a vampire recoiling from a sunbeam. "Let me ask the wife," he continues, and now *I'm* confused.

"Hey, dear, you wanna go carve up some tasty elk?"

You've got to be kidding me, I think. It's 2:30 in the morning and it's cold outside and it's warm in bed and it's 2:30 in the morning and it's cold outside and I've never carved up an actual whole elk before and I'm a little bit scared and it's 2:30 in the morning.

"Ahhhhh . . . yeah, I guess, you wanna?" I steel myself for his response. Maybe he doesn't wanna, and then I could say, "We could've had elk meat this year, but . . ."

But he says "sure."

We stumble into warm, unimportant clothes and Ranger looks at us dazed, he stretches, shakes, turns in a circle and plops back onto his bed.

We added our names to the Sheriff's Department Roadkill List last year after discovering it was "a thing" from another hunter and had already turned down a couple of previous calls for side-of-the-road deer when we weren't available for a speedy response. We had no real excuse this time, and we were told it was a cow elk about a 15-minute drive away. It was my hunting season. I had a tag for a cow elk (not necessary for a roadkill) and hadn't seen a single sign of one, probably because I was hunting up in the mountains during daylight, not along county roads at night.

As we approach the mile marker we were told she was near, Mike slows his truck and I strain my eyes to find her. My butterflies wake up. My time has finally come to put my YouTube and book-learnin' to practical use. For the past couple of years I'd watched and re-watched Fred Eichler's YouTube video on the "gutless method" of quartering an elk until I knew I could do it when the time came.

The time had come.

"There she is," I point to the body conveniently lying on her side just off the road. Mike parks his truck so the headlights illuminate the scene. It's about 3 a.m. and not as cold as it could be. She's gorgeous. She's young.

And she's still warm. Her open eyes, lovely long-lashed soft brown, disinterested, nonjudgmental, show no sign of fear or struggle. I stroke the so-soft fur along her neck and thank her for what I'm about to do. A knot catches in my throat and I can't look into her eyes again.

With two short-bladed knives at the ready, my Havalon and Mike's Gerber, I raise her right front leg.

"Here, hold this up," I direct Mike. I take a deep breath and visualize Eichler as he makes short, fast cuts until the shoulder peels away from its blade. It works, and Mike deposits our first quarter on a clean tarp.

The right hind quarter is more difficult because of its size and the bones involved and the fact that I'm cutting near the gut. After another deep breath—I'm sweating at this point—I do exactly what I've burned into my brain, find the hip socket, think briefly about Mike's new titanium hip, shake that thought from my head, and with Mike holding up the weight of it, after several more slices along the curvature of the butt bone (that's the technical name), we have a beautiful hind quarter.

"What's next?" Mike asks.

"Backstrap," I say, "and I'd like to keep the pelt."

After cutting the hide up the belly, I have Mike pull back on the pelt while I release it with quick slices from the warm body. I'm surprised by how easily it peels away. When I get over the backbone, I'm ready to liberate the first backstrap, that long, tender meat along the length of the backbone. Piece of cake.

Now I'm nervous because I want the tenderloin. To do that, I've got to make an incision below the bottom rib, reach my hand inside, grab it, and cut it on either end from its connective tissue. I'm afraid of puncturing the gut with my knife. Despite the headlights, we're really working in the dark, and I can't seem to feel what I'm after.

My hand slides between the gut and the ribs and I marvel at the warmth and silky smoothness. I push back against the abdomen and continue my search for the most prized piece, but to no avail.

"Let's roll her onto the other side," I tell Mike, though I feel guilty I've failed this task. As we roll her over, a car creeps by and then speeds off toward the pass to Aspen.

"Bet they've never seen something like this before," Mike says, and we laugh at what a sight we must be— nighttime knife-wielding roadside butchers eerily illuminated in the headlights. "At least if they call the police they'll already know about the roadkill notification."

By the time the next two quarters and backstrap are liberated, I feel like I've just competed in a wrestling match. I'm sweating bullets. I've used muscle fibers that have been dormant for years. I must get the tenderloin from this side.

I reach my hand in again and hear the sound of air escaping.

"Oh, shit!"

"You didn't cut the intestines, did you?" Mike jumps back with an expression of foul anticipation.

But there's no smell. My hand probes up higher into the ribcage and I feel something flat. "I think it was a lung. You should really feel in here," I tell him, and he does. "I think if you'll use both hands and pull back on the gut, I can find it." He pulls the now-bulging gut away from the backbone and my hand finds the treasure. I cut out the large-baked-potato-size tenderloin.

After bagging and storing the meat and pelt in the back of the truck, we look at what remains on the side of the road.

"We should probably pull it farther back into the brush," Mike suggests, and this turns into no easy task. Even with all we've removed, it takes the two of us with arms around the weighty head to pull what remains of the cow into a place she won't be spotted from the road.

It's still dark when we get home and we're stupid tired. Our garage is cold. We work together to hang the four quarters from hooks in the rafters and the place is transformed into the freezer scene from *Rocky*.

Ranger is happy to see us and even happier to sniff our blood-stained boots. I shower and fall into bed, knowing my real work—skinning, butchering, packaging and freezing all that meat—is just beginning.

"Bet you never thought you'd be doing stuff like *this* 33 years ago," Mike says.

"Nope. Never in a million years."

I close my eyes and know I'll never forget a single moment from the past few hours. And I'll never forget those lovely brown eyes.

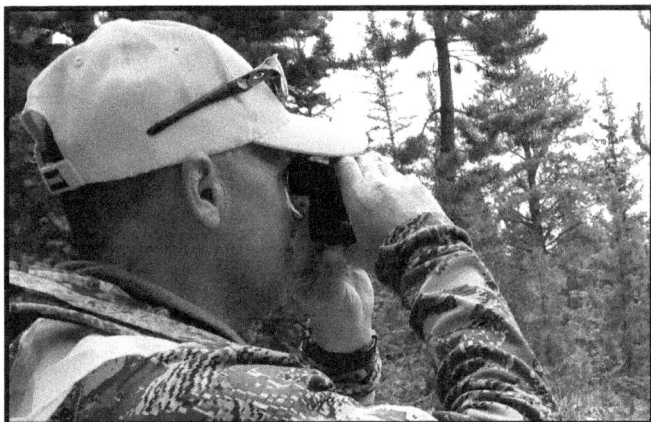

9: NEXT, PLEASE!

"If some animals are good at hunting and others are suitable for hunting, then the gods must clearly smile on hunting." ~Aristotle

With summer just starting in Leadville, Colorado (June 2017), it's hard to believe hunting season is just around the corner! We've just learned that Mike drew a cow tag for this year, but I didn't! That's okay. I'm already brushing up on my quartering skills. We're down to just a few packages of fajita meat in the freezer from last fall's roadkill, so I'm looking forward to restocking soon! This will surely be the year!

If you're a hunter or hiker (hunting for breathtaking scenery), you should consider purchasing **and learning how to use** a GPS (Global Positioning System). It will help immensely when you need to remember where you left your tasty meat, or if you've lost yourself in the excitement of the hunt, it will help you find your way back home!

Sally, a fellow hunter and writer, recently provided me with a Top 10 list of GPS devices and a link to an article with more information about each. Here's what she sent:

In the books I read as a child, the hero, well anyone who was hunting, did so with a bow and arrow. They navigated from memory or by using the sun and the stars (not at the same time naturally). Today, it's a little different, but a large part of me loves the idea of ditching technology and going out, me versus the moose mano a mano or well, womano a moose.

Now we have small children and I have a tech obsessed husband, the question has not been what technology to use, but which type of each gadget available. One of the ones he loves most is the GPS device, as someone who is great at navigating without a map, using one is a disaster in the making, so I'll give it to him, GPS are useful because they tell me where on the map I am and how to get to my destination. So, after a bit of trial and error, we've worked through and reviewed the top 10 available right now, which are:

1. *eTrex (Garmin)*
2. *Montana 680 Touchscreen GPS (Garmin)*
3. *Rhino 750 (Garmin)*

4. *Oregon 650t GPS (Garmin)*
5. *Garmin 64st*
6. *eTrex 10 (Garmin)*
7. *eTrex 20x (Garmin)*
8. *DeLorme InReach SE*
9. *Back Track G2 (Bushnell)*
10. *Foretex 401 (Garmin)*

That's just the list. I've put together the pros and cons of each as well as a review in this article covering the top 10 handheld GPS devices at: http://www.10hunt.com/best-handheld-gps/.

Please check out Sally's article! I know that after some of my hunting expeditions, I could benefit from knowing how to use a GPS, but so far, Mike hasn't steered me wrong! I plan to enjoy many more years of hunting with my best friend—my husband.

10: "HOOKED!"

"Last year I went fishing with Salvador Dali. He was using a dotted line. He caught every other fish."
~Steven Wright

For all you fisher-folks out there (including all you fisher-folk-newbies), here's a BONUS story: A fish tale designed to reel you in!

It was too late by the time I realized that I hadn't asked the most crucial question: "What do I do if I actually catch something?" My husband and I had agreed to go camping and fishing with some friends, and I was really excited about finally learning how to catch and prepare my own meal.

Having spent years in the army—during which time I had travelled the world, jumped out of airplanes, and fired many types of weapons—it was a source of embarrassment that by the age of 53 I had never actually gone fishing.

So I posted a "Gone Fishing" status update on my Facebook page, packed up the camper for a two day adventure and headed south with my man and dreams of landing the big one.

Day One was all about learning how to string the rod, place the bait and cast. After opening the bale without having my finger on the line a couple times, I was able to practice the art of patience required to untangle and re-reel the explosions of silky filament. Although I felt a surge of hopeful excitement while reeling in a small branch (it sure felt like something fighting at the end of my line!), none of us caught more than clumps of moss that day.

Nevertheless, we basked in the sun and were happy to be away from the responsibilities of home, and I felt a Zen-like satisfaction in watching the line arch away from me before hearing the satisfying "plunk" of the lure as it disappeared in the river.

I woke on Day Two, elated, from a dream of catching a huge fish. In my dream there were four enormous tunas, all different colors, lined up sardine-style in a swimming pool. I cast my line into the pool and instantly pulled dinner for fifty out of the water. It was simple! And what a way to start my second day of fishing—with a prophetic vision!

The morning was considerably colder than the previous day and the clouds were ominous, but I knew what I had to do. Our new location looked much more promising; there were about seven others already downstream from the spot we selected and at least one line had action. I selected my spot to the far right of the group because with only one day of casting under my belt, I was not yet feeling like a pro. My location choice also had me standing on a steeply angled embankment, but it felt nice to dig my heels into the spongy sand.

Within five minutes of launching my first fat worm into the river, I let out a loud "OOOOOH!"—much louder than I should have, because now I had the attention of every fisherperson down river from me. This was no branch. I started reeling in my catch with vociferous encouragement from hubby, who told me to reel it in faster. How I wish I had had the presence of mind to send him up the hill for a camera, because the sight which ensued could very well have launched my career as a comedic actor.

I marveled at the beauty of my rainbow trout as it neared shore; it was the size of a football, and my dream of feeding the masses was about to come true. "Hurry up! Get it out of the water!" my husband directed. He was as excited as I was about my first catch. In a scene that would have inspired Hemingway, I pulled my treasure from the river . . . and then wasn't quite sure what to do next.

All eyes on me now, I responded to shouts of "Bring it up here!" by swiveling to my left away from the water with my fish swinging like a tetherball at the end of the line, and then I promptly slipped on the sand in my attempt to run up the slope. My three pounds of prime fish-fry smacked into the sandy hill, the impact releasing it from the hook and freeing it to roll back down the hill and into the water to safety.

But he wasn't going to get away that easily. Dropping my rod, I dove on top of the flopping fish, determined to catch it and carry it up to my now anxious husband and friends. In my frenzy to win this battle (remember the slippery slope upon which I once stood?), I ended up rolling ass-over-teakettle into the cold river, all the while wrestling with my wily rival. Up to the armpits of my fleece jacket in the cold current, arms flailing wildly as my slippery supper sought his escape, I did everything I could to re-capture my catch . . . but to no avail; "Charlie" was in his element now, and his enthusiasm to live another day thwarted my best efforts to wrangle him back to shore.

I crawled from the water, empty-handed and giddy with the exertion of my unconventional fishing technique, and was the first one to start laughing. Soon, all of the stunned spectators were giggling, and it took quite a while before they returned to their own pursuits. I insisted on staying and continuing to try my luck at another catch, shivering uncontrollably for about another hour before we all returned to our campground to fry up our friend's smaller catch.

Some of my friends squealed, "Oh! That poor fish!" when they heard my tale, but I know the truth. When my little Houdini got back to his school that day, his story of the 130-pound Great White that he had let escape made him King of the Sea, if only for a moment. Thanks, little guy, for the thrill, but watch your tail...I now know what to do should our paths cross again!

For more photos, go to: http://leadvillelaurel.com/hooked/

ACKNOWLEDGMENTS

Would I be redundant in acknowledging the man who keeps me on my toes year after challenge-filled year? I think not. Thank you, Mike McHargue. Without you, there would be no love in my hunting stories and no hunting stories to tell! And I have a really good feeling that *this* will be "the year"!

Nick McHargue, my fabulous firstborn, thank you for your patience whenever I ask, "Want me to read it to you?" You know it's a rhetorical question, and I appreciate your generosity. I'll never tire of your puns. Thank you as well for the BLOOK idea.

Jake McHargue, my spectacular secondborn, thank you too for adding to the pun pile and for looking for ways to help me spread the word about my work. You encouraged me years ago to manage my own blog, and now I have material for many blooks.

Carol Bellhouse, thank you for encouraging me to create a stand-alone publication with my hunting stories. Your suggestion relieved me from creating a *MONSTER BLOOK*!

And Erin Sue Grantham—hunter, writer, storyteller— thank you for telling me *years* ago that I should compile my blog posts into a book! This one's right up your alley!

John Stewart, thank you for countless hours of weapons training, and Brad and Rachele Palmer, thank you for doing your best to school me on proper fishing techniques! I know I'll never live down the day the fish reeled *me* in!

ABOUT THE AUTHOR

Award-winning author Laurel McHargue, a 1983 graduate of The United States Military Academy at West Point, was raised in Braintree, Massachusetts, but somehow found her way to the breathtaking elevation of Leadville, Colorado, where she has taught and currently lives with her husband and Ranger, the German Shepherd.

Find Laurel on Amazon!
You might enjoy her other publications:

> **The Hare, Raising Truth**
> **"Miss?"**
> **Waterwight: Book I of the Waterwight Series**
> **Haikus Can Amuse: 366 Haiku Starters**
> **Hai CLASS ku**

Laurel's goal is to author as many books as possible in genres of every type. This is the first of this type!

Visit her at www.leadvillelaurel.com where she blogs about life, real and imagined, and sign up for her non-spamming, mid-monthly newsletter!

~ ~ ~ If you enjoyed this blook, please consider ~ ~ ~
telling others about it in a review!

www.ingramcontent.com/pod-product-compliance
Lightning Source LLC
LaVergne TN
LVHW051803080426
835511LV00018B/3395